Contents

KT-116-074

Words appearing in the text in bold,
like this, are explained in the Glossary.

 Find out more about how things are
made at www.heinemannexplore.co.uk

What is in a bicycle?

Many children enjoy riding a bicycle.
Bicycles are made of different materials.
Each material helps to make the bicycle
strong and to work well.

plastic

steel

rubber

How Is a Bicycle Made?

Angela Royston

Heinemann
LIBRARY

Young
Explorer

www.heinemann.co.uk/library

Visit our website to find out more information about Heinemann Library books.

To order:
☎ Phone 44 (0) 1865 888066
📄 Send a fax to 44 (0) 1865 314091
💻 Visit the Heinemann Bookshop at www.heinemann.co.uk/library to browse our catalogue and order online.

First published in Great Britain by Heinemann Library, Halley Court, Jordan Hill, Oxford OX2 8EJ, part of Harcourt Education. Heinemann is a registered trademark of Harcourt Education Ltd.

Editorial: Lucy Thunder and Louise Galpine
Design: Jo Hinton-Malivoire and AMR
Illustration: Art Construction
Picture Research: Melissa Allison and Debra Weatherley
Production: Camilla Smith

Originated by RMW
Printed and bound in China by South China Printing Company

The paper used to print this book comes from sustainable resources

ISBN 0 431 05047 3 (hardback)
09 08 07 06 05
10 9 8 7 6 5 4 3 2 1

ISBN 0 431 05054 6 (paperback)
10 09 08 07 06
10 9 8 7 6 5 4 3 2 1

British Library Cataloguing in Publication Data
Royston, Angela
How is a bicycle made?
629.2'272
A full catalogue record for this book is available from the British Library.

Acknowledgements
The Publishers would like to thank the following for permission to reproduce photographs: Alamy/Henry Westheim pp. **18**, **19**; Corbis pp.**15**, **28** (Charles O'Rear); Corbis/Royalty-free p.**14**; George Robinson p.**16**; Getty Images p.**11**; Getty Images/Photodisc p.**10**; Harcourt Education Ltd /Tudor Photography pp.**13**, **17**; Robert Harding Picture Library p.**12** (J Miller); Stockfile pp.**4**, **6**, **7**, **8**, **9**, **20**, **21**, **22**, **23**, **25**, **26**, **27** (Steven Behr); Trek Bicycle Corporation pp. **24**, **28**, **29**.

Cover photograph of bicycles reproduced with permission of Harcourt Education Ltd/Tudor Photography.

The Publishers would like to thank Brian Buckle for his assistance in the preparation of this book.

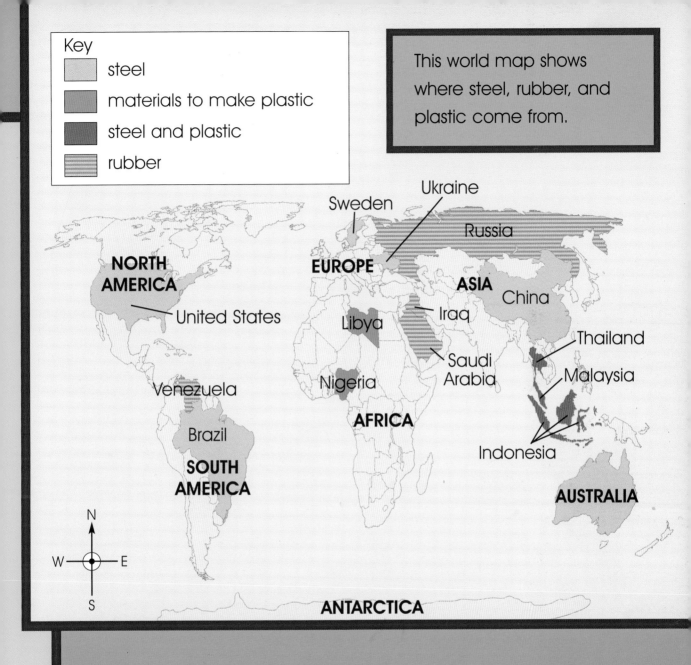

Key
- steel
- materials to make plastic
- steel and plastic
- rubber

This world map shows where steel, rubber, and plastic come from.

Sweden · Ukraine · Russia

NORTH AMERICA — United States

EUROPE

ASIA · China

Libya · Iraq · Thailand

Venezuela · Nigeria · Saudi Arabia · Malaysia

Brazil · AFRICA · Indonesia

SOUTH AMERICA · AUSTRALIA

N W E S

ANTARCTICA

Most bicycles are made mainly of **steel**, **rubber** and **plastic**. These materials come from many different parts of the world.

Who makes bicycles?

Lots of different **companies** make bicycles. Each company has a factory. Many people work for the company. Workers in the factory make the bicycles.

Some people work in the company's offices.
Workers **design** new bicycles. Other workers
buy the materials needed to make
the bicycles.

Designing a bicycle

Designers think of new kinds of bicycle. They draw the designs on a computer or on paper. They look for ways of making the bicycle work better.

Experts test examples over rough ground.

Experts build and test examples of the best bicycles. Then the **company** decides which ones to make and sell.

Making steel

The **frame** of the bicycle is made mainly of **steel**. Steel is made from **iron ore**. Iron ore is dug out of the ground and then it is heated in a **furnace**.

The furnace makes the iron ore so hot it becomes liquid.

Different metals are added to liquid iron to make steel. Steel is stronger than iron. Hot steel is poured into **moulds** to make steel tubes.

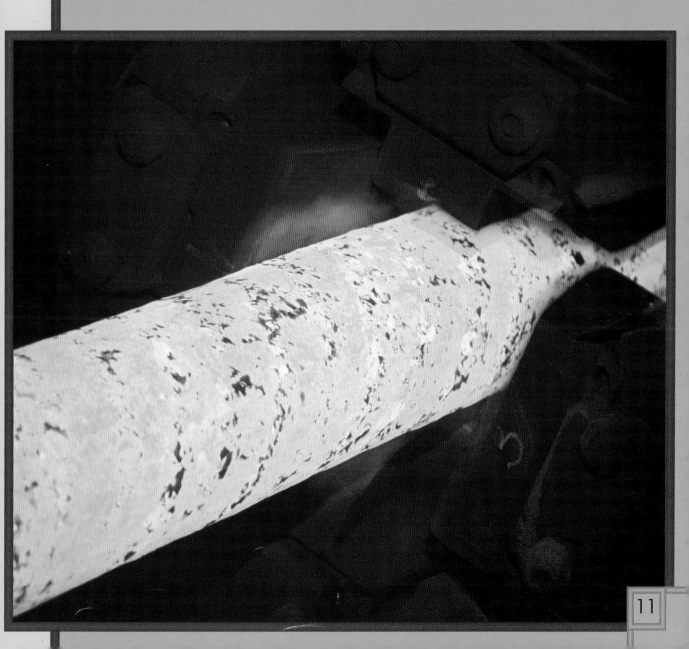

Making rubber tyres

Rubber comes from rubber trees. When the bark of a rubber tree is cut, a thick liquid called latex oozes out. The liquid is collected in cups.

This rubber tree in Malaysia has been grown to produce latex.

There are many
different sizes of tyre.

In the rubber factory, latex is made into
rubber. A tyre factory buys **bales** of
rubber and turns them into tyres.

Where plastic comes from

Plastic is made from **oil**. Oil is found deep under the ground. Oil workers drill down to reach the oil. The oil is taken to an oil **refinery**.

The oil refinery separates the oil into petrol and other liquids. Most petrol is burned in cars, but some is made into plastic.

These small pieces of plastic are made from oil.

Making the saddle and wheel guards

Plastic is cheap and can be made into different shapes. Plastic pellets are fed into different-shaped **moulds** to make the bicycle saddle and the wheel guards.

Plastic saddles are shaped inside a mould.

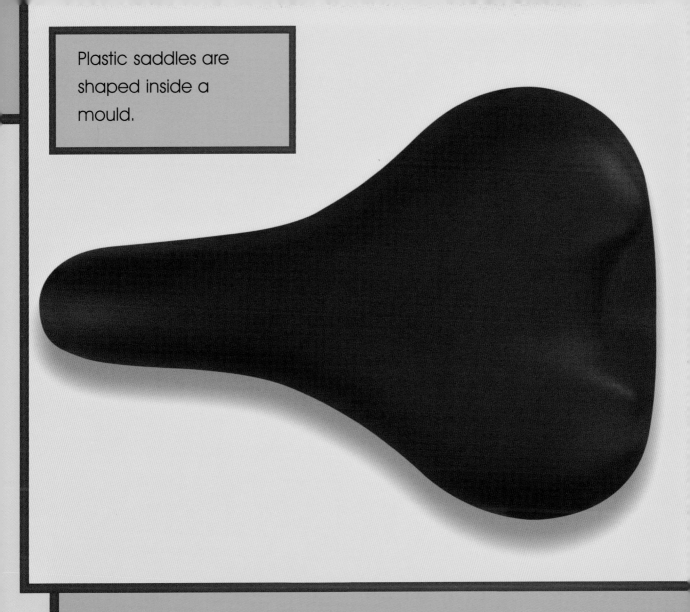

The plastic pellets melt inside the moulds and are mixed with a **dye** to colour them. When the moulds have cooled, they are taken off.

Making the frame

Lorries take all the different parts of the bicycle to the bicycle factory. A machine in the factory cuts the steel tubes. Another machine bends them into the right shapes.

A worker **welds** the different pieces together to make the frame. This means that the ends of the tubes are heated until they melt together.

The welding light is so bright the worker must wear a mask.

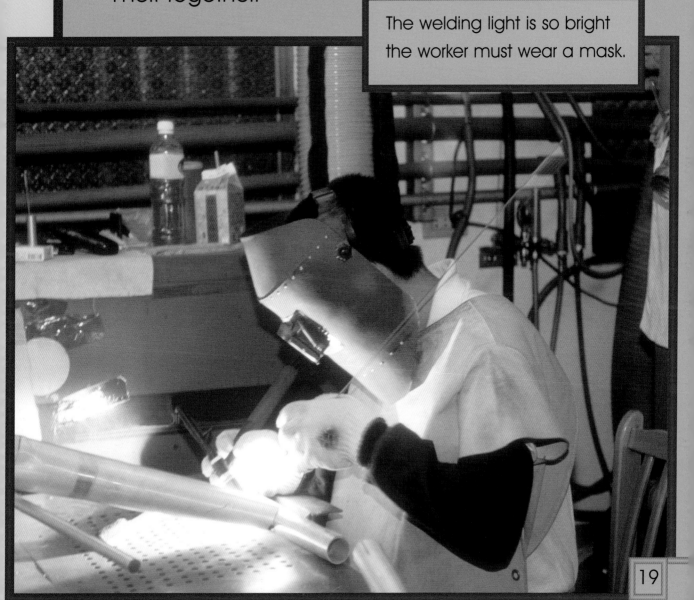

Making the wheels

A wheel has a hub, spokes, a rim, and a tyre. The spokes are put into the hub. Then a worker fits the spokes into the rim.

hub

spokes

rim

A worker fits the tyre around the edge of the rim.

The tyre has a thin tube inside called an inner tube. The inner tube is filled with air. The rubber and the air make the bike comfortable to ride.

Putting it all together

The steel frame is sprayed with paint in the paint shop. When the paint is dry, the frame is put onto a **conveyor belt**.

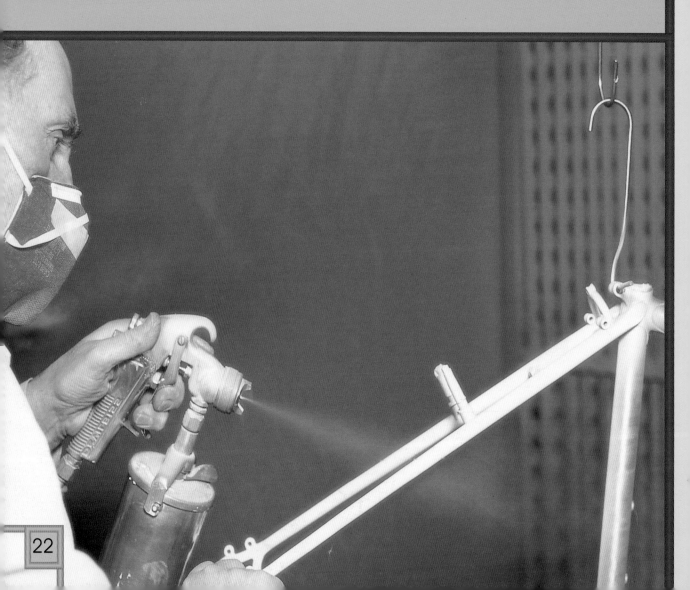

The frame moves along the conveyor belt.
Workers and machines add all the parts to
the bicycle, one by one.

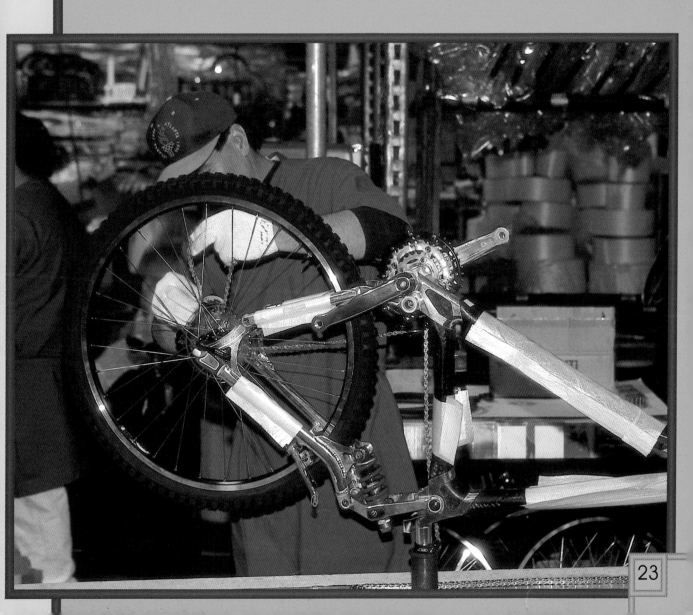

The finished bicycle

When the bicycle is finished, it is tested to make sure that everything works well. The brakes are tested, as well as the wheels and pedals.

The finished bicycles are stored in a
warehouse. When a shop needs more
bicycles to sell, the shop orders them
from the bicycle **company**.

Selling the bicycles

A lorry takes the new bicycles from the **warehouse** to different shops. Here people can look at many different bicycles before deciding which one to buy.

Some of the money you pay for a bicycle goes to the bicycle **company**. They use some of this money to make more bicycles.

From start to finish

A bicycle is made mainly of **steel**. Steel is made from **iron ore**.

The steel is made into tubes.

The tubes are bent and joined together to make the frame.

The frame is put on a **conveyor belt**. The other parts are added piece by piece.

A closer look

Every bicycle has the name of the bicycle **company** printed on it. The tyres are also printed with the name of the company that made them.

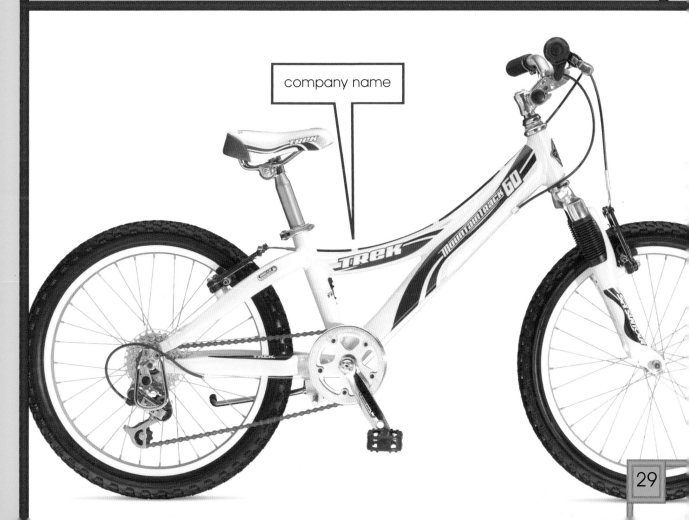

company name

Glossary

bale large amount of something tied up to make a bundle

company group of people who work together

conveyor belt machine that carries things on a long loop from one place to another

design decide how an object or machine will look

designer person who decides how an object will look

dye substance that gives plastic, paint, or cloth its colour

expert someone who knows all about a topic

furnace very hot oven

iron ore rock that contains iron

mould hollow container

oil liquid that forms under the ground

plastic material made from oil or coal

refinery place where oil is separated into petrol and other liquids

rubber bendy, waterproof material made from the juice of rubber trees

steel kind of metal made from iron ore

warehouse building where things are stored

welded joined together by heating the ends of two pieces of metal

Places to visit

Catalyst, Widnes: hands-on and interactive exploration of how the science of chemistry affects our everyday lives;
www.catalyst.org.uk

Coventry Transport Museum, Coventry: includes cars as well as over 200 bicycles;
www.transport-museum.com

Eureka! The Museum for Children, Halifax: interactive exhibits exploring the world of science;
www.eureka.org.uk

Glasgow Science Centre, Glasgow: fun way to learn more about science and technology;
www.glasgowsciencecentre.org

National Cycle Collection, Llandrindod Wells: includes almost every kind of bicycle you can think of;
www.cyclemuseum.org.uk

The Science Museum, London: many special exhibitions as well as the museum's historic collection;
www.sciencemuseum.org.uk

Scienceworks, Melbourne, Australia;
www.scienceworks.museum.vic.gov.au

Index